LIVING LIFE ON PURPOSE
PROGRAM™

A TRANSFORMATIONAL LIFE-ALIGNMENT WORKBOOK

DR. JONATHAN K. JEFFERSON

Written By: Dr. Jonathan K. Jefferson
Designed & Edited By: Aaron C. Butler

ISBN: 9781967082834
Library of Congress Control Number: 2025925019

Printed in the United States of America

BookButler Publishing Company
Upper Marlboro, MD 20774
TheBookButler.com

BookButler Publishing Company titles may be purchased in bulk for educational, business, fundraising, or sales promotional use.

For more information, please email: info@thebookbutler.com

THIS WORKBOOK BELONGS TO

_____

INTRODUCTION

Living on purpose is the foundation of transformational leadership.

Before you can lead others with clarity, you must first understand what drives you, energizes you, and aligns with who you are becoming.

The Living Life On Purpose Program™ helps you identify what matters most in the eight key areas of your life and create a clear plan for intentional, purpose-aligned living. This workbook serves as the practical companion to **Transformational Leadership: Unleashing Your Full Potential**, guiding you from awareness to action through reflection, prioritization, and daily alignment.

Take your time. Be honest. Lean into the process. Your journey toward clarity, balance, and purpose starts here.

HOW TO USE THIS WORKBOOK

This workbook is designed to help you apply the **Living Life On Purpose Program**™ and align your daily life with your deepest values, goals, and priorities.

Each section guides you through:

- **Wants Discovery** — exploring what you desire in the eight key areas of life
- **Core Wants Prioritization** — identifying what matters most
- **Daily Alignment Tools** — designing and tracking your Ideal On-Purpose Day
- **Purpose & Vision Worksheets** — defining how you will live on purpose
- **Living on Purpose Reflections** — capturing insights as you grow

Tip:
Dedicate a little time each week to reflection and review.
Alignment happens through consistency, not intensity.

HOW THIS WORKBOOK FITS THE TRANSFORMATIONAL LEADERSHIP FRAMEWORK

The **Living Life On Purpose Program**™ aligns with the four pillars of Transformational Leadership:

AWARENESS

Know Yourself
to Lead
Yourself

ALIGNMENT

Bring Your Life,
Values, and Vision
Into Sync

ACTION

Lead With Purpose
Through
Consistent Habits

ACCOUNTABILITY

Sustain Your
Growth Over
Time

Table of Contents

SECTION I

Living on Purpose: The Foundation

Discover what it truly means to live with clarity, intention, and alignment.

Before designing your Ideal On-Purpose Day or starting the 28-Day Alignment journey, this section helps you understand the mindset and foundation required to begin living life on purpose.

Chapter 1: What Does It Mean to Live on Purpose?

Living on purpose means choosing direction over drift. It's the intentional practice of aligning your values, priorities, and daily actions with the person you are becoming — not the person your schedule, circumstances, or habits have allowed you to be.

When you live on purpose, you move from reacting to life to leading your life. Purpose becomes a filter for decisions, relationships, opportunities, and boundaries. Instead of scattering your time and energy across competing demands, you begin directing them toward what truly matters.

Living on purpose isn't about perfection. It's about clarity.

It's about recognizing where your life feels aligned — and where it doesn't. It's a commitment to honest reflection and small, consistent steps toward a more intentional way of living.

In the **Living Life On Purpose Program™**, you'll explore the eight key areas that shape your overall well-being and fulfillment. You'll identify what you want, prioritize what's essential, and design a life anchored in purpose rather than pressure.

Before you can lead others effectively, you must lead yourself with intention.

Purpose is the starting point.

REFLECTION: CHECKING YOUR ALIGNMENT

Take a few quiet moments to reflect on where your life feels aligned — and where it feels out of sync.

When do you feel most "on purpose" in your daily life?

_____

_____

_____

Where do you feel misaligned, drained, or distracted?

_____

_____

_____

What areas of your life currently feel the most meaningful?

_____

_____

_____

WORKSHEET: MY CURRENT ALIGNMENT SNAPSHOT

Rate each statement from 1 (Not true for me) to 5 (Very true for me)

STATEMENT	1	2	3	4	5
I make decisions based on my values.	○	○	○	○	○
My daily actions reflect what matters most.	○	○	○	○	○
I feel clarity about where my life is headed.	○	○	○	○	○
I feel energized by the way I live.	○	○	○	○	○
I set boundaries that protect my time and well-being.	○	○	○	○	○

What did your ratings tell you about your current alignment?

_____

_____

_____

_____

LIVING ON PURPOSE
Chapter Reflection

WHAT YOU LEARNED:

Living on purpose begins with awareness. This chapter helped you take an honest look at where your life feels aligned — and where it doesn't. Purpose becomes clearer when you slow down long enough to notice what energizes you, what drains you, and what deserves your attention.

YOUR INSIGHT

What stood out to you the most from this chapter?

_____

_____

_____

YOUR ALIGNMENT ACTION

What is one small change you can make this week to live more intentionally?

_____

_____

_____

YOUR MOMENTUM

How will you hold yourself accountable for this change?

_____

_____

_____

Chapter 2: Breaking Free from Kryptonite Syndrome

Kryptonite Syndrome describes the patterns, habits, and pressures that drain your energy and keep you from living with clarity, purpose, and alignment. It's the cycle of running hard but never feeling caught up, wanting change but not knowing where to begin. When Kryptonite Syndrome is active, you may feel overwhelmed, exhausted, frustrated, or stuck — even when you're achieving or serving others.

Living on purpose requires identifying what is weakening your momentum. In this chapter, you will explore where Kryptonite Syndrome shows up in your life and begin breaking free from the patterns that hold you back.

Are you suffering from KRYPTONITE syndrome?

K *killing yourself while*
R *running but not getting to the finish line*
Y *yearning for something more, but*
P *procrastinating, not knowing where to start*
T *trying to get to the next level, but*
O *overwhelmed by all of your responsibilities*
N *needing a change in your life, but*
I *ignoring your dreams*
T *troubled that you are not being heard*
E *exasperated, ready to give up!!!*

REFLECTION: WHERE IS YOUR ENERGY BEING DRAINED?

Take a few quiet moments to reflect on the areas of your life where you feel depleted, overwhelmed, or stuck. Awareness of these energy drains is the first step to breaking free from Kryptonite Syndrome.

Which parts of your life feel the most exhausting or overwhelming right now?

_____

_____

_____

_____

When do you notice yourself running but not making meaningful progress?

_____

_____

_____

What responsibilities or habits consume your energy without moving you toward your purpose?

_____

_____

_____

WORKSHEET: IDENTIFYING YOUR KRYPTONITE PATTERNS

Check all that apply to your experience:

KRYPTONITE PATTERN	CHECK
I feel like I'm always "on," with little time to rest.	☐
I say yes to things that don't align with my values.	☐
I'm busy, but not productive in meaningful ways.	☐
I struggle to set boundaries with people or responsibilities.	☐
I feel stuck in routines that no longer serve me.	☐
I procrastinate on things that matter most.	☐

What patterns stand out the most?

_____

_____

_____

LIVING ON PURPOSE
Chapter Reflection

WHAT YOU LEARNED:

Kryptonite Syndrome is not a lack of effort — it's a lack of alignment. This chapter helped you identify the habits, pressures, and patterns that drain your energy and keep you from living intentionally. Awareness is the first step toward reclaiming your time, clarity, and focus.

YOUR INSIGHT

What did you notice about your Kryptonite patterns?

_____

_____

_____

YOUR ALIGNMENT ACTION

What is one small shift you can make this week to reduce energy drains?

_____

_____

_____

YOUR MOMENTUM

Who or what will help you stay accountable as you break free from these patterns?

_____

_____

_____

SECTION II

Discovering What You Want

Gain clarity about the eight key areas that shape your life, well-being, and personal fulfillment.

Before you identify your Core Wants or begin aligning your daily habits, this section guides you through exploring what truly matters and uncovering the desires that will anchor your purpose.

Chapter 3: Exploring the Eight Life Areas

Living on purpose requires clarity about all the parts of your life—not just the areas that demand your attention today. The eight life areas give you a holistic view of your well-being, your responsibilities, and your desires. When one area is ignored, the others eventually feel the impact. When each area is acknowledged, you create space for balance, growth, and alignment.

In this chapter, you will explore the eight life areas that form the foundation of the **Living Life On Purpose Program™.** This exploration will prepare you to identify your Wants Lists and ultimately discover the Core Wants that shape your purpose.

REFLECTION: UNDERSTANDING YOUR LIFE AREAS

Take a moment to consider each area of your life and how much attention, energy, or intention you currently give it.

Which life areas feel strong and supported right now?

_____

_____

_____

Which areas feel overlooked or underdeveloped?

_____

_____

_____

Which area do you feel most motivated to improve? Why?

_____

_____

_____

Which life area has been the hardest for you to prioritize, and what has made it challenging?

_____

_____

_____

WORKSHEET: YOUR LIFE AREAS OVERVIEW

Below is a quick snapshot of the eight life areas you will explore more deeply in the next section.

Rate your current satisfaction in each area from 1 (Not satisfied) to 5 (Very satisfied).

LIFE AREA	1	2	3	4	5
Physical | Health | Recreation	○	○	○	○	○
Financial | Material	○	○	○	○	○
Social | Community	○	○	○	○	○
Intellectual | Mental	○	○	○	○	○
Spiritual	○	○	○	○	○
Family	○	○	○	○	○
Vocational | Career	○	○	○	○	○
Other _____	○	○	○	○	○

Which areas stood out to you?

_____

_____

_____

LIVING ON PURPOSE
Chapter Reflection

WHAT YOU LEARNED:

Clarity begins with awareness. This chapter helped you examine the eight key life areas that shape your overall well-being and alignment. When you understand where you feel strong and where you feel stretched, you can begin to make intentional choices that support a more purposeful life.

YOUR INSIGHT

What did you learn about yourself as you explored the eight life areas?

_____

_____

_____

YOUR ALIGNMENT ACTION

Which life area will you focus on improving this week?

_____

_____

_____

YOUR MOMENTUM

What is one small step you can take to support that area?

_____

_____

_____

Chapter 4: Identifying Your Core Wants

Once you've explored what you want across the eight life areas, the next step is to determine which desires matter most right now. Not every want carries the same weight. Some reflect short-term preferences, while others reveal deeper needs, motivations, and values. Your Core Wants are the desires that anchor your purpose, direct your decisions, and shape the life you are working to build.

In this chapter, you will use the Core Want Tournament to prioritize the wants in each life area. This simple process helps you uncover the one want that will have the greatest impact on your alignment, fulfillment, and progress.

REFLECTION: PRIORITIZING WHAT MATTERS MOST

Before you begin the Core Want Tournament, take a moment to think about how you typically make decisions and set priorities.

When you consider your wants, what factors influence your priorities most?

_____

_____

_____

Which life area feels the hardest to prioritize? Why?

_____

_____

_____

Which area feels the clearest or easiest to prioritize?

_____

_____

_____

What do you hope to gain from identifying your Core Wants?

_____

_____

_____

WORKSHEET: WANTS LIST PATTERN

Before identifying your Core Want, take a moment to reflect on what you truly desire in this area of your life.

List Your Wants Using the Alternating Pattern:

As you write your Wants List, it's important to follow the alternating number pattern shown on the page. This pattern is a core part of the **Living Life On Purpose Program™** and prepares your list for the Core Want Tournament.

Write your first want at the top, your second at the bottom, your third back at the top, and continue alternating until all of your wants are listed.

Here is the alternating pattern: 1 / 3 / 5 / 7 / 9 / 10 / 8 / 6 / 4 / 2.

Why This Pattern is Important

Using this approach:
- Prevents your wants from clustering in a way that biases your decisions later
- Ensures you naturally compare wants from the top and bottom of your list
- Balances your list for the tournament activity that follows
- Helps you see a wider range of desires before prioritizing

Instructions

Write freely — do not filter, judge, or prioritize yet. You may list as many wants as you have — **do not limit yourself to ten.** If you have fewer or more than ten wants, that's perfectly fine — simply continue the alternating pattern until you are finished.

Note: Use this process for each life area to identify your Core Want.

PHYSICAL HEALTH RECREATION

1	
3	
5	
7	
9	
10	
8	
6	
4	
2	

FINANCIAL MATERIAL

1	
3	
5	
7	
9	
10	
8	
6	
4	
2	

SOCIAL COMMUNITY

1	
3	
5	
7	
9	
10	
8	
6	
4	
2	

INTELLECTUAL MENTAL

1	
3	
5	
7	
9	
10	
8	
6	
4	
2	

SPIRITUAL

1	
3	
5	
7	
9	
10	
8	
6	
4	
2	

FAMILY

1	
3	
5	
7	
9	
10	
8	
6	
4	
2	

VOCATIONAL CAREER

1	
3	
5	
7	
9	
10	
8	
6	
4	
2	

OTHER

1	
3	
5	
7	
9	
10	
8	
6	
4	
2	

WORKSHEET: CORE WANT TOURNAMENT INSTRUCTIONS

Now that you've created your Wants Lists using the alternating pattern, it's time to identify the one want in each Life Area that matters most right now.

The Core Want Tournament works just like a sports bracket — you compare your wants in pairs and advance the "winner" until only one remains.

This process helps you cut through preferences and discover the desire that carries the greatest meaning, motivation, and impact for your life.

NOTE: You will repeat this process for all 8 Life Areas.

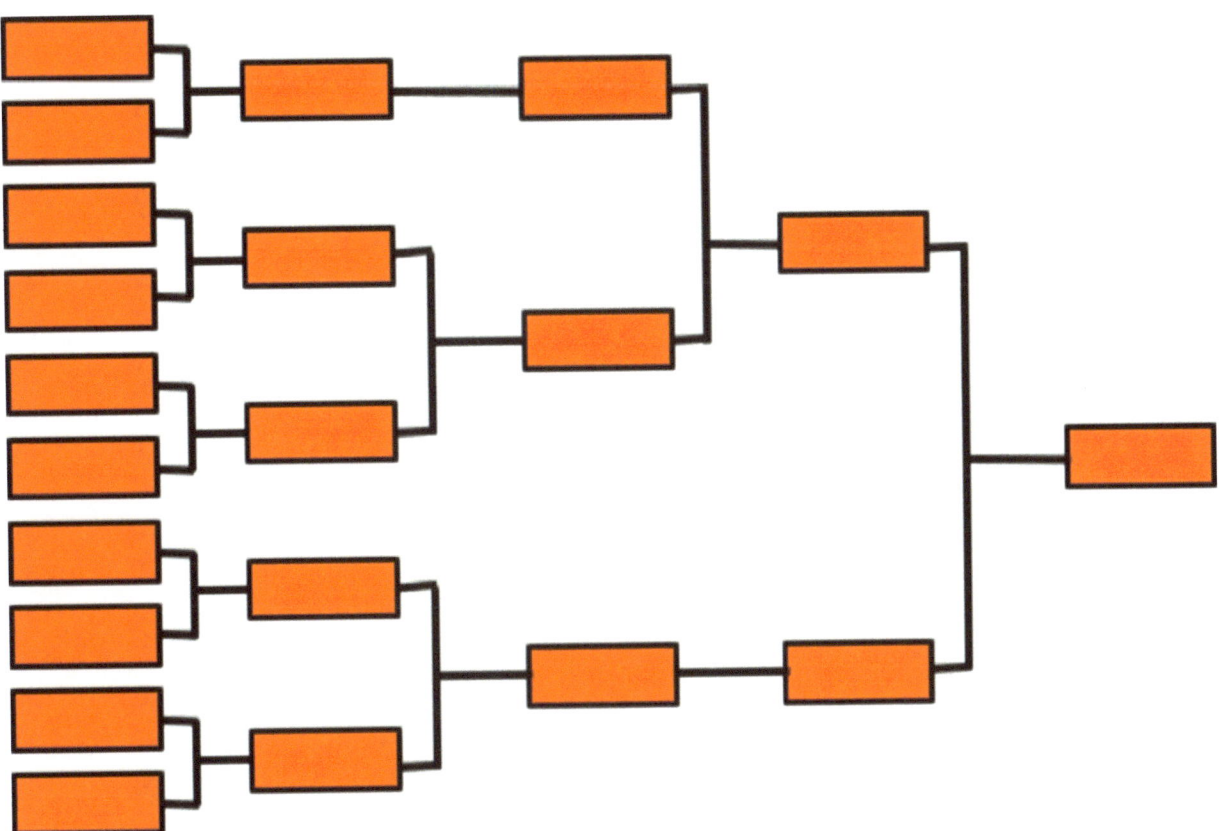

CORE WANT SUMMARY

Use this page to record the Core Want you identified in each of the eight life areas. These Core Wants will guide your Ideal On-Purpose Day and your 28-Day Alignment plan.

LIFE AREA	CORE WANT
Physical / Health / Recreation	
Financial / Material	
Social / Community	
Intellectual / Mental	
Spiritual	
Family	
Vocational / Career	
Other	

LIVING ON PURPOSE
Chapter Reflection

WHAT YOU LEARNED:

Prioritization brings clarity. This chapter helped you distinguish between surface-level desires and the deeper wants that shape your purpose. When you know what truly matters, decision-making becomes easier and alignment becomes possible.

YOUR INSIGHT

What did you learn about yourself as you identified your Core Wants?

_____

_____

_____

YOUR ALIGNMENT ACTION

Which Core Want feels the most urgent or meaningful to act on right now?

_____

_____

_____

YOUR MOMENTUM

What first step can you take to honor that Core Want this week?

_____

_____

_____

SECTION III

Creating Your On-Purpose Life

Begin translating your clarity into action.

Before you design your 28-Day Alignment plan or define your purpose statement, this section guides you in shaping your Ideal On-Purpose Day and building the habits that support intentional living.

Chapter 5: Designing Your Ideal On-Purpose Day

Your Ideal On-Purpose Day represents the life you are working toward — a day where your time, attention, and energy reflect what matters most. This exercise is not about creating a "perfect" day. It's about gaining clarity on how you want to live, what you want to prioritize, and where you want your time to go.

Designing your Ideal On-Purpose Day helps you see the gap between where you are and where you want to be. Over time, small, intentional choices can bring your real life closer to your ideal one.

REFLECTION: HOW DO YOU CURRENTLY SPEND YOUR TIME?

Before designing your ideal day, take a moment to consider how your time is currently used.

What parts of your current day feel aligned with your Core Wants?

_____

_____

_____

What parts of your day feel rushed, stressful, or out of balance?

_____

_____

_____

What activities or habits take up time but don't support the life you want?

_____

_____

_____

How would you like your daily rhythm to feel — energized, calm, structured, flexible, focused?

_____

_____

_____

WORKSHEET: CREATE YOUR IDEAL ON-PURPOSE DAY

Use the chart below to map out your ideal 24-hour day. Start by choosing your wake-up time and bedtime, then allocate hours or percentages to each Core Want area.

LIFE AREA	CORE WANT	CORE WANT	TIME ALLOCATION
Wake-Up Time	_____	
Physical / Health / Recreation		
Financial / Material		
Social / Community		
Intellectual / Mental		
Family		
Spiritual		
Vocational / Career		
Other _____		
Bedtime	_____	

Remember: This is an ideal — not a requirement. Over time, your daily reality can move closer to your Ideal On-Purpose Day through small, consistent shifts.

LIVING ON PURPOSE
Chapter Reflection

WHAT YOU LEARNED:

Your daily rhythm shapes your purpose. This chapter helped you visualize a day that aligns with your Core Wants and reveals what a purpose-driven life looks like in real time. When you design your day with intention, you create the foundation for consistent, meaningful progress.

YOUR INSIGHT

What stood out to you as you designed your Ideal On-Purpose Day?

_____

_____

_____

YOUR ALIGNMENT ACTION

What small change can be made this week to bring your current day closer to your ideal day?

_____

_____

_____

YOUR MOMENTUM

What habit or commitment will help you stay aligned?

_____

_____

_____

Living on purpose requires consistency. Small, intentional actions taken over time create lasting change. The 28-Day Alignment System helps you practice your Ideal On-Purpose Day in real life by tracking how you spend your time, what habits support your purpose, and where adjustments are needed.

This system is not about perfection — it's about awareness. Over 28 days, you will observe patterns, celebrate progress, and gently correct areas that pull you out of alignment. The more clarity you gain, the more intentional your days become.

REFLECTION: PREPARING FOR DAILY ALIGNMENT

Before beginning the 28-Day Alignment System, reflect on what alignment means for you right now.

What habits or routines currently support your Ideal On-Purpose Day?

_____

_____

_____

What habits or routines tend to pull you away from your Core Wants?

_____

_____

_____

What do you hope to learn about yourself through daily tracking?

_____

_____

_____

WORKSHEET: HOW TO USE THE 28-DAY DAILY ALIGNMENT TEMPLATE

The template you'll use for each day includes three simple sections:

1. Core Want Priorities
List your Core Want for each life area.
These remind you what you're aligning your day around.

2. Time Allocation
Record how much time or energy you devoted to each area.
This helps you compare your real day to your Ideal On-Purpose Day.

3. Reflection Notes
Capture key observations:
- What felt aligned?
- What felt out of sync?
- What energized you?
- What drained you?

You may complete one page per day, or use it weekly by summarizing your patterns. Either approach builds awareness and momentum.

A full set of **28 Daily Alignment Templates** is included in the Appendix for your month-long alignment journey.

Sample Template

DAILY ALIGNMENT TEMPLATE

DAY _____ DATE _____

LIFE AREA | CORE WANT	CORE WANT	TIME ALLOCATION
Wake-Up Time	_____	
Physical / Health / Recreation		
Financial / Material		
Social / Community		
Intellectual / Mental		
Family		
Spiritual		
Vocational / Career		
Other		
Bedtime	_____	

This template is for DAILY use, unlike the Ideal Day template which is conceptual.

DAILY NOTES | REFLECTIONS

_____

_____

_____

_____

_____

_____

LIVING ON PURPOSE
Chapter Reflection

WHAT YOU LEARNED:

Alignment comes from intention, not intensity. This chapter helped you prepare for the daily practice of paying attention to how you spend your time and how closely your actions reflect your purpose. Consistency, honesty, and gentle course-correction create real transformation.

YOUR INSIGHT

What did today's reflection teach you about your daily patterns?

_____

_____

_____

YOUR ALIGNMENT ACTION

What is one habit you will focus on strengthening during your 28-day journey?

_____

_____

_____

YOUR MOMENTUM

How will you stay committed to this process when the days feel busy or challenging?

_____

_____

_____

SECTION IV

Defining Your Purpose

Clarify the deeper meaning behind your Core Wants, values, and daily choices.

Before creating your Purpose, Mission, Vision, and Values statements, this section guides you in reflecting on who you are, what you stand for, and the life you are committed to building.

Chapter 7: Establishing Your Life Purpose Statement

Your life purpose is the foundation of living on purpose. It answers the question: **"Why do I exist?"**

Purpose brings clarity to your decisions, strength to your commitments, and meaning to your daily life. It is not about titles, roles, or accomplishments. It is about who you are at your core and how you are called to serve.

In this chapter, you will begin shaping your Purpose, Mission, Vision, and Values — the elements that guide how you live, lead, and make intentional choices every day.

REFLECTION: UNDERSTANDING YOUR INNER DIRECTION

Before writing your purpose statement, take a moment to reflect deeply on your identity, motivations, and impact.

When do you feel most alive and connected to who you truly are?

_____

_____

_____

What strengths or gifts do others consistently recognize in you?

_____

_____

_____

What burdens your heart or pulls your attention toward helping others?

_____

_____

_____

WORKSHEET: PURPOSE, MISSION, VISION & VALUES

PURPOSE – BEING

Your purpose is expressed in the statement:

"I exist to serve by _____."

VISION – SEEING

Your vision describes where you are going and the future you see for your life.

My Vision: _____

_____

_____

_____

_____

_____

MISSION – DOING

Your mission reflects how you live out your purpose in your daily life and in specific areas.

My Mission: _____

_____

_____

_____

_____

_____

VALUES — CHOOSING

Your values define the principles and behaviors that guide your choices and character.

My Core Values: _____

_____

_____

_____

_____

_____

_____

_____

COMMITMENTS — BECOMING

Your commitments represent how you will honor your Core Wants and live out your purpose.

My Commitments: _____

_____

_____

_____

_____

_____

_____

_____

LIVING ON PURPOSE
Chapter Reflection

WHAT YOU LEARNED:

Purpose brings direction. This chapter guided you toward expressing why you exist, what drives you, and how you intend to live out your calling. When you define your Purpose, Mission, Vision, and Values, you gain a clear compass for making meaningful decisions and aligning your life with who you were created to be.

YOUR INSIGHT

What did you discover about yourself while writing your purpose statement?

_____

_____

_____

YOUR ALIGNMENT ACTION

What is one way you can honor your purpose in your daily life this week?

_____

_____

_____

YOUR MOMENTUM

What will help you stay grounded in your purpose during challenging moments?

_____

_____

_____

Chapter 8: Bringing Your Purpose to Life

A purpose statement becomes powerful only when it moves from the page into your daily decisions. Living on purpose means allowing your Purpose, Mission, Vision, and Values to guide how you use your time, respond to challenges, build relationships, and pursue opportunities.

Bringing your purpose to life is not about grand gestures — it's about consistent choices. When you act in alignment with your purpose, even small steps create momentum. Purpose becomes visible in how you lead, serve, communicate, rest, and grow.

In this chapter, you will explore practical ways to live your purpose every day.

REFLECTION: WHAT DOES PURPOSE LOOK LIKE IN DAILY LIFE?

Take a moment to reflect on how your purpose can shape the way you live, work, and interact with others.

What daily behaviors or habits would reflect your purpose more clearly?

_____

_____

_____

What behaviors or habits feel out of alignment with your purpose?

_____

_____

_____

What small shifts could you make this week to embody your purpose more fully?

_____

_____

_____

WORKSHEET: APPLYING PURPOSE TO DAILY LIFE

Use this page to translate your Purpose, Mission, Vision, and Values into practical action.

LIVING MY PURPOSE

How I will live out my purpose today:

_____

_____

LIVING MY MISSION

One action I can take that reflects my mission:

_____

_____

LIVING MY VISION

One step that moves me closer to the future I envision:

_____

_____

LIVING MY VALUES

One value I will intentionally practice today:

_____

_____

LIVING MY COMMITMENTS

One commitment I want to honor this week:

_____

_____

LIVING ON PURPOSE
Chapter Reflection

WHAT YOU LEARNED:

Purpose becomes powerful through action. This chapter helped you identify how your Purpose, Mission, Vision, and Values can show up in your everyday choices. When your actions reflect the life you are building, you create consistency, clarity, and alignment.

YOUR INSIGHT

What did you learn about how your purpose influences your daily decisions?

_____

_____

_____

YOUR ALIGNMENT ACTION

What is one practical step you will take this week to live your purpose intentionally?

_____

_____

_____

YOUR MOMENTUM

Who or what will help you stay grounded in your purpose as you continue this journey?

_____

_____

_____

SECTION V

Continuing Your Transformation

Continue strengthening the habits, clarity, and purpose you've developed throughout this workbook.

Before reviewing your progress or planning your next steps, this section supports your long-term alignment and helps you carry your transformation forward with confidence and intention.

Chapter 9: Staying Aligned Beyond the Workbook

Your transformation doesn't end when you complete this workbook — it continues as you practice living with clarity, intention, and purpose. Alignment is a lifelong process. There will be seasons of growth, seasons of challenge, and seasons of recalibration. What matters most is your commitment to return to your purpose, your Core Wants, and the habits that help you live on purpose every day.

This chapter offers guidance for maintaining your alignment as life evolves, responsibilities shift, and new opportunities emerge. Your purpose grows as you grow, and these tools will help you stay grounded, aware, and intentional.

REFLECTION: STAYING GROUNDED IN YOUR PURPOSE

Take a moment to reflect on what you need in order to remain aligned in the weeks and months ahead.

What practices or habits help you feel centered and aligned?

_____

_____

_____

What early signs tell you that you're drifting out of alignment?

_____

_____

_____

Who supports your growth, accountability, and well-being?

_____

_____

_____

What will you prioritize in the next 30 days to stay connected to your purpose?

_____

_____

_____

How do you want your future self to describe the way you lived during this season?

_____

_____

_____

_____

WORKSHEET: BUILDING YOUR ALIGNMENT PLAN

Use this page to map out your next steps for living on purpose beyond the workbook.

Habits to Continue
These habits support your clarity, purpose, or momentum:

_____

_____

_____

Habits to Adjust
These habits need refinement, boundaries, or balance:

_____

_____

_____

Habits to Release

These habits drain energy or pull you out of alignment:

_____

_____

_____

People Who Support My Purpose

List mentors, peers, or supporters who help you stay aligned:

1 _____

2 _____

3 _____

4 _____

5 _____

My Next 3 Alignment Actions

1 _____

_____

2 _____

_____

3 _____

_____

LIVING ON PURPOSE
Chapter Reflection

WHAT YOU LEARNED:

Transformation is sustained through intention and awareness. This chapter encouraged you to identify the habits, supports, and choices that help you remain aligned with your purpose as life continues to unfold. Your journey doesn't end here — it expands as you keep choosing purpose every day.

YOUR INSIGHT

What did you discover about what you need to stay aligned?

_____

_____

_____

YOUR ALIGNMENT ACTION

What is one specific action you will take this month to reinforce your alignment?

_____

_____

_____

YOUR MOMENTUM

Who or what will help you stay accountable as you continue living on purpose?

_____

_____

_____

Your growth doesn't end with completing this workbook — it evolves as you apply the principles of living on purpose to the changing seasons of your life. Transformation is ongoing. As your responsibilities shift, your opportunities expand, and your identity deepens, your purpose becomes clearer and your alignment becomes stronger.

In this chapter, you'll revisit the foundational ideas from Transformational Leadership: Unleashing Your Full Potential and explore how to sustain momentum, course-correct when needed, and recommit to your purpose with clarity and intention.

This is your reminder: You are not just completing a program — you are stepping into a lifestyle of transformation.

Connection to the Transformational Leadership Model
Your growth continues through the TL pillars:
Awareness → Alignment → Action → Accountability.
These same pillars support your long-term purpose and transformation.

REFLECTION: STAYING CONNECTED TO YOUR LEADERSHIP JOURNEY

Use these questions to reconnect with your purpose, leadership identity, and long-term vision.

What leadership principles from Transformational Leadership have made the greatest impact on you?

_____

_____

How do you want your leadership — at home, work, and in your community — to reflect your purpose?

_____

_____

_____

WORKSHEET: STRENGTHENING YOUR LONG-TERM ALIGNMENT

When You Fall Off — How to Course-Correct

Everyone loses alignment occasionally. What matters is noticing it early.

My early signs of misalignment:

_____

_____

_____

_____

_____

How I will reset when I drift:

_____

_____

_____

_____

Quarterly Core Want Review

Your Core Wants may evolve as your life changes.

Date of my next review: _____

What I will revisit:
- Wants List
- Core Wants
- Ideal On-Purpose Day
- Values & Commitments

Staying Connected to Your Purpose

Choose the practices that will help you remain centered:

☐ Weekly reflection

☐ Morning routine | grounding practice

☐ Journaling

☐ Accountability partner

☐ Monthly alignment check

☐ Other:_____

Your Transformation Leadership Connection

How do the concepts from Transformational Leadership guide your next steps?

_____

_____

_____

_____

_____

_____

NOTES | REFLECTIONS

_____

_____

_____

_____

_____

_____

LIVING ON PURPOSE
Chapter Reflection

WHAT YOU LEARNED:

Transformation is a continuous journey, not a one-time event. This chapter helped you connect the principles of purpose, alignment, and leadership to your long-term growth. As you revisit your Core Wants, adjust your habits, and recommit to your values, you continue to unleash your full potential.

YOUR INSIGHT

What did you realize about your ongoing growth and leadership?

_____

_____

_____

YOUR ALIGNMENT ACTION

What is one intentional step you will take over the next 30 days to continue your journey?

_____

_____

_____

YOUR MOMENTUM

What systems, people, or habits will help sustain your transformation?

_____

_____

_____

A Closing Message

You've taken an important step in your transformational journey. By completing this workbook, you've done more than reflect on your life — you've chosen clarity, alignment, and intentional growth. That choice alone separates those who drift from those who lead.

There will be days ahead when purpose feels clear and days when alignment feels harder to hold. That's normal. What matters is your willingness to pause, reflect, and reconnect with the Core Wants, values, and purpose you identified here. Transformation is not a one-time event — it is a lifestyle of returning to what matters most.

As you move forward, remember this: **You cannot lead others well if you are not leading yourself with intention.** Your purpose, your habits, and your alignment shape the way you present yourself at home, at work, and in your community. When you live on purpose, you give others permission and inspiration to do the same.

I encourage you to revisit this workbook quarterly. Your Core Wants will evolve. Your commitments will deepen. Your vision will expand. Each time you return to your purpose with honesty and humility, you strengthen the leader within.

Thank you for trusting this process. Thank you for choosing growth. And thank you for stepping into the life you were created to live.
Keep going. Keep growing. Keep living on purpose.

— Dr. Jonathan K. Jefferson

When you drift → return to your purpose.
When you grow → update your tools.
When in doubt → simplify back to your Core Wants.

FINAL CALL TO ACTION

Your Next Step: Keep Leading on Purpose

Transformation doesn't end here — it continues with the choices you make every day.

Revisit your Core Wants each quarter. Re-align when you drift. Celebrate progress with gratitude.

And above all, **keep showing up for the life you were created to live.**

If you ever lose clarity, return to this workbook.

If you ever lose momentum, return to your purpose.

And if you ever need support, connect with the tools, community, and coaching designed to help you live and lead on purpose.

You are not done — you are just getting started.

Living Life On Purpose Program™
Quick Reference Guide

The Eight Life Areas

Reflect honestly on each area of your life:
- Physical / Health / Recreation
- Financial / Material
- Social / Community
- Intellectual / Mental
- Spiritual
- Family
- Vocational / Career
- Other (your choice)

Kryptonite Syndrome

Identify what drains your energy or pulls you off-purpose:
- Overcommitment
- Poor boundaries
- Unaligned habits
- Emotional or mental exhaustion
- "Busy but not productive" cycles

Wants Lists

Write down everything you desire in each life area **without filtering.**
- This reveals deeper patterns behind what you truly want.
- Allows you to see your desires clearly before prioritizing or refining them.

Core Wants Tournament

Prioritize each Wants List to identify your **Core Want** per life area:
1. Pair your wants
2. Compare them
3. Narrow the winners
4. Choose the final Core Want

Core Wants Summary

Capture your top want in each life area. These Core Wants become anchors for decisions, boundaries, and habits.

Ideal On-Purpose Day

Map out a full 24-hour day that reflects your Core Wants. Consider:
- Wake/sleep times
- Energy rhythms
- Key priorities
- How you want your day to feel

Your Ideal On-Purpose Day becomes your blueprint for intentional living.

28-Day Alignment System

Track your daily alignment for 28 days:
- Time spent per Life Area
- What energized you
- What drained you
- Degree of alignment
- Small adjustments

Focus on **awareness,** not perfection.

Purpose / Mission / Vision / Values

Purpose — Being
"I exist to serve by _____."

Mission — Doing
How do you live out your purpose daily?

Vision — Seeing
The future you are working toward.

Values — Choosing
Principles that guide your decisions.

Quarterly Alignment Check

Every 90 days, revisit and refine:
- Wants Lists
- Core Wants
- Ideal On-Purpose Day
- Values & Commitments
- Alignment patterns

Growth is cyclical — return often.

LIVING ON PURPOSE IS A LIFESTYLE
Use these tools to align your days, decisions, actions, and relationships with what matters most.

APPENDIX

Daily Alignment Template | 28 Days

DAILY ALIGNMENT TEMPLATE | DAY 1

DATE _____

LIFE AREA	CORE WANT	CORE WANT	TIME ALLOCATION
Wake-Up Time	_____	
Physical / Health / Recreation		
Financial / Material		
Social / Community		
Intellectual / Mental		
Family		
Spiritual		
Vocational / Career		
Other		
Bedtime	_____	

This template is for DAILY use, unlike the Ideal Day template which is conceptual.

DAILY NOTES | REFLECTIONS

_____

_____

_____

_____

_____

_____

DAILY ALIGNMENT TEMPLATE | DAY 2

DATE _____

LIFE AREA	CORE WANT	CORE WANT	TIME ALLOCATION
Wake-Up Time	_____	
Physical / Health / Recreation		
Financial / Material		
Social / Community		
Intellectual / Mental		
Family		
Spiritual		
Vocational / Career		
Other		
Bedtime	_____	

This template is for DAILY use, unlike the Ideal Day template which is conceptual.

DAILY NOTES | REFLECTIONS

_____

_____

_____

_____

_____

_____

DAILY ALIGNMENT TEMPLATE | DAY 3

DATE _____

LIFE AREA	CORE WANT	CORE WANT	TIME ALLOCATION
Wake-Up Time	_____	
Physical / Health / Recreation		
Financial / Material		
Social / Community		
Intellectual / Mental		
Family		
Spiritual		
Vocational / Career		
Other		
Bedtime	_____	

This template is for DAILY use, unlike the Ideal Day template which is conceptual.

DAILY NOTES | REFLECTIONS

_____

_____

_____

_____

_____

_____

DAILY ALIGNMENT TEMPLATE | DAY 4

DATE _____

LIFE AREA	CORE WANT	CORE WANT	TIME ALLOCATION
Wake-Up Time	_____	
Physical / Health / Recreation		
Financial / Material		
Social / Community		
Intellectual / Mental		
Family		
Spiritual		
Vocational / Career		
Other		
Bedtime	_____	

This template is for DAILY use, unlike the Ideal Day template which is conceptual.

DAILY NOTES | REFLECTIONS

_____

_____

_____

_____

_____

_____

DAILY ALIGNMENT TEMPLATE | DAY 5

DATE _____

LIFE AREA	CORE WANT	CORE WANT	TIME ALLOCATION
Wake-Up Time	_____	
Physical / Health / Recreation		
Financial / Material		
Social / Community		
Intellectual / Mental		
Family		
Spiritual		
Vocational / Career		
Other		
Bedtime	_____	

This template is for DAILY use, unlike the Ideal Day template which is conceptual.

DAILY NOTES | REFLECTIONS

_____

_____

_____

_____

_____

_____

DAILY ALIGNMENT TEMPLATE | DAY 6

DATE _____

LIFE AREA	CORE WANT	CORE WANT	TIME ALLOCATION
Wake-Up Time	_____	
Physical / Health / Recreation		
Financial / Material		
Social / Community		
Intellectual / Mental		
Family		
Spiritual		
Vocational / Career		
Other		
Bedtime	_____	

This template is for DAILY use, unlike the Ideal Day template which is conceptual.

DAILY NOTES | REFLECTIONS

_____

_____

_____

_____

_____

_____

DAILY ALIGNMENT TEMPLATE | DAY 7

DATE _____

LIFE AREA	CORE WANT	CORE WANT	TIME ALLOCATION
Wake-Up Time	_____	
Physical / Health / Recreation		
Financial / Material		
Social / Community		
Intellectual / Mental		
Family		
Spiritual		
Vocational / Career		
Other		
Bedtime	_____	

This template is for DAILY use, unlike the Ideal Day template which is conceptual.

DAILY NOTES | REFLECTIONS

_____

_____

_____

_____

_____

_____

DAILY ALIGNMENT TEMPLATE | DAY 8

DATE _____

LIFE AREA	CORE WANT	CORE WANT	TIME ALLOCATION
Wake-Up Time	_____	
Physical / Health / Recreation		
Financial / Material		
Social / Community		
Intellectual / Mental		
Family		
Spiritual		
Vocational / Career		
Other		
Bedtime	_____	

This template is for DAILY use, unlike the Ideal Day template which is conceptual.

DAILY NOTES | REFLECTIONS

_____

_____

_____

_____

_____

_____

DAILY ALIGNMENT TEMPLATE | DAY 9

DATE _____

LIFE AREA	CORE WANT	CORE WANT	TIME ALLOCATION
Wake-Up Time	_____	
Physical / Health / Recreation		
Financial / Material		
Social / Community		
Intellectual / Mental		
Family		
Spiritual		
Vocational / Career		
Other		
Bedtime	_____	

This template is for DAILY use, unlike the Ideal Day template which is conceptual.

DAILY NOTES | REFLECTIONS

_____

_____

_____

_____

_____

_____

DAILY ALIGNMENT TEMPLATE | DAY 10

DATE _____

LIFE AREA	CORE WANT	CORE WANT	TIME ALLOCATION
Wake-Up Time	_____	
Physical / Health / Recreation		
Financial / Material		
Social / Community		
Intellectual / Mental		
Family		
Spiritual		
Vocational / Career		
Other		
Bedtime	_____	

This template is for DAILY use, unlike the Ideal Day template which is conceptual.

DAILY NOTES | REFLECTIONS

_____

_____

_____

_____

_____

_____

DAILY ALIGNMENT TEMPLATE | DAY 11

DATE _____

LIFE AREA	CORE WANT	CORE WANT	TIME ALLOCATION
Wake-Up Time	_____	
Physical / Health / Recreation		
Financial / Material		
Social / Community		
Intellectual / Mental		
Family		
Spiritual		
Vocational / Career		
Other		
Bedtime	_____	

This template is for DAILY use, unlike the Ideal Day template which is conceptual.

DAILY NOTES | REFLECTIONS

_____

_____

_____

_____

_____

_____

DAILY ALIGNMENT TEMPLATE | DAY 12

DATE _____

LIFE AREA	CORE WANT	CORE WANT	TIME ALLOCATION
Wake-Up Time	_____	
Physical / Health / Recreation		
Financial / Material		
Social / Community		
Intellectual / Mental		
Family		
Spiritual		
Vocational / Career		
Other		
Bedtime	_____	

This template is for DAILY use, unlike the Ideal Day template which is conceptual.

DAILY NOTES | REFLECTIONS

_____

_____

_____

_____

_____

_____

DAILY ALIGNMENT TEMPLATE | DAY 13

DATE _____

LIFE AREA | CORE WANT	CORE WANT	TIME ALLOCATION
Wake-Up Time	_____	
Physical / Health / Recreation		
Financial / Material		
Social / Community		
Intellectual / Mental		
Family		
Spiritual		
Vocational / Career		
Other		
Bedtime	_____	

This template is for DAILY use, unlike the Ideal Day template which is conceptual.

DAILY NOTES | REFLECTIONS

_____

_____

_____

_____

_____

DAILY ALIGNMENT TEMPLATE | DAY 14

DATE _____

LIFE AREA | CORE WANT	CORE WANT	TIME ALLOCATION
Wake-Up Time	_____	
Physical / Health / Recreation		
Financial / Material		
Social / Community		
Intellectual / Mental		
Family		
Spiritual		
Vocational / Career		
Other		
Bedtime	_____	

This template is for DAILY use, unlike the Ideal Day template which is conceptual.

DAILY NOTES | REFLECTIONS

_____

_____

_____

_____

_____

_____

DAILY ALIGNMENT TEMPLATE | DAY 15

DATE _____

LIFE AREA	CORE WANT	CORE WANT	TIME ALLOCATION
Wake-Up Time	_____	
Physical / Health / Recreation		
Financial / Material		
Social / Community		
Intellectual / Mental		
Family		
Spiritual		
Vocational / Career		
Other		
Bedtime	_____	

This template is for DAILY use, unlike the Ideal Day template which is conceptual.

DAILY NOTES | REFLECTIONS

_____

_____

_____

_____

_____

_____

DAILY ALIGNMENT TEMPLATE | DAY 16

DATE _____

LIFE AREA	CORE WANT	CORE WANT	TIME ALLOCATION
Wake-Up Time	_____	
Physical / Health / Recreation		
Financial / Material		
Social / Community		
Intellectual / Mental		
Family		
Spiritual		
Vocational / Career		
Other		
Bedtime	_____	

This template is for DAILY use, unlike the Ideal Day template which is conceptual.

DAILY NOTES | REFLECTIONS

_____

_____

_____

_____

_____

_____

DAILY ALIGNMENT TEMPLATE | DAY 17

DATE _____

LIFE AREA	CORE WANT	CORE WANT	TIME ALLOCATION
Wake-Up Time	_____	
Physical / Health / Recreation		
Financial / Material		
Social / Community		
Intellectual / Mental		
Family		
Spiritual		
Vocational / Career		
Other		
Bedtime	_____	

This template is for DAILY use, unlike the Ideal Day template which is conceptual.

DAILY NOTES | REFLECTIONS

_____

_____

_____

_____

_____

_____

DAILY ALIGNMENT TEMPLATE | DAY 18

DATE _____

LIFE AREA	CORE WANT	CORE WANT	TIME ALLOCATION
Wake-Up Time	_____	
Physical / Health / Recreation		
Financial / Material		
Social / Community		
Intellectual / Mental		
Family		
Spiritual		
Vocational / Career		
Other		
Bedtime	_____	

This template is for DAILY use, unlike the Ideal Day template which is conceptual.

DAILY NOTES | REFLECTIONS

_____

_____

_____

_____

_____

_____

DAILY ALIGNMENT TEMPLATE | DAY 19

DATE _____

LIFE AREA	CORE WANT	CORE WANT	TIME ALLOCATION
Wake-Up Time	_____	
Physical / Health / Recreation		
Financial / Material		
Social / Community		
Intellectual / Mental		
Family		
Spiritual		
Vocational / Career		
Other		
Bedtime	_____	

This template is for DAILY use, unlike the Ideal Day template which is conceptual.

DAILY NOTES | REFLECTIONS

_____

_____

_____

_____

_____

_____

DAILY ALIGNMENT TEMPLATE | DAY 20

DATE _____

LIFE AREA	CORE WANT	CORE WANT	TIME ALLOCATION
Wake-Up Time	_____	
Physical / Health / Recreation		
Financial / Material		
Social / Community		
Intellectual / Mental		
Family		
Spiritual		
Vocational / Career		
Other		
Bedtime	_____	

This template is for DAILY use, unlike the Ideal Day template which is conceptual.

DAILY NOTES | REFLECTIONS

_____

_____

_____

_____

_____

_____

DAILY ALIGNMENT TEMPLATE | DAY 21

DATE _____

LIFE AREA	CORE WANT	CORE WANT	TIME ALLOCATION
Wake-Up Time	_____	
Physical / Health / Recreation		
Financial / Material		
Social / Community		
Intellectual / Mental		
Family		
Spiritual		
Vocational / Career		
Other		
Bedtime	_____	

This template is for DAILY use, unlike the Ideal Day template which is conceptual.

DAILY NOTES | REFLECTIONS

_____

_____

_____

_____

_____

_____

DAILY ALIGNMENT TEMPLATE | DAY 22

DATE _____

LIFE AREA | CORE WANT	CORE WANT	TIME ALLOCATION
Wake-Up Time	_____	
Physical / Health / Recreation		
Financial / Material		
Social / Community		
Intellectual / Mental		
Family		
Spiritual		
Vocational / Career		
Other		
Bedtime	_____	

This template is for DAILY use, unlike the Ideal Day template which is conceptual.

DAILY NOTES | REFLECTIONS

_____

_____

_____

_____

_____

_____

DAILY ALIGNMENT TEMPLATE | DAY 23

DATE _____

LIFE AREA | CORE WANT	CORE WANT	TIME ALLOCATION
Wake-Up Time	_____	
Physical / Health / Recreation		
Financial / Material		
Social / Community		
Intellectual / Mental		
Family		
Spiritual		
Vocational / Career		
Other		
Bedtime	_____	

This template is for DAILY use, unlike the Ideal Day template which is conceptual.

DAILY NOTES | REFLECTIONS

_____

_____

_____

_____

_____

_____

DAILY ALIGNMENT TEMPLATE | DAY 24

DATE _____

LIFE AREA	CORE WANT	CORE WANT	TIME ALLOCATION
Wake-Up Time	_____	
Physical / Health / Recreation		
Financial / Material		
Social / Community		
Intellectual / Mental		
Family		
Spiritual		
Vocational / Career		
Other		
Bedtime	_____	

This template is for DAILY use, unlike the Ideal Day template which is conceptual.

DAILY NOTES | REFLECTIONS

_____

_____

_____

_____

_____

_____

DAILY ALIGNMENT TEMPLATE | DAY 25

DATE _____

LIFE AREA	CORE WANT	CORE WANT	TIME ALLOCATION
Wake-Up Time	_____	
Physical / Health / Recreation		
Financial / Material		
Social / Community		
Intellectual / Mental		
Family		
Spiritual		
Vocational / Career		
Other		
Bedtime	_____	

This template is for DAILY use, unlike the Ideal Day template which is conceptual.

DAILY NOTES | REFLECTIONS

_____

_____

_____

_____

_____

_____

DAILY ALIGNMENT TEMPLATE | DAY 26

DATE _____

LIFE AREA	CORE WANT	CORE WANT	TIME ALLOCATION
Wake-Up Time	_____	
Physical / Health / Recreation		
Financial / Material		
Social / Community		
Intellectual / Mental		
Family		
Spiritual		
Vocational / Career		
Other		
Bedtime	_____	

This template is for DAILY use, unlike the Ideal Day template which is conceptual.

DAILY NOTES | REFLECTIONS

_____

_____

_____

_____

_____

_____

DAILY ALIGNMENT TEMPLATE | DAY 27

DATE _____

LIFE AREA	CORE WANT	CORE WANT	TIME ALLOCATION
Wake-Up Time	_____	
Physical / Health / Recreation		
Financial / Material		
Social / Community		
Intellectual / Mental		
Family		
Spiritual		
Vocational / Career		
Other		
Bedtime	_____	

This template is for DAILY use, unlike the Ideal Day template which is conceptual.

DAILY NOTES | REFLECTIONS

_____

_____

_____

_____

_____

_____

DAILY ALIGNMENT TEMPLATE | DAY 28

DATE _____

LIFE AREA	CORE WANT	CORE WANT	TIME ALLOCATION
Wake-Up Time	_____	
Physical / Health / Recreation		
Financial / Material		
Social / Community		
Intellectual / Mental		
Family		
Spiritual		
Vocational / Career		
Other		
Bedtime	_____	

This template is for DAILY use, unlike the Ideal Day template which is conceptual.

DAILY NOTES | REFLECTIONS

_____

_____

_____

_____

_____

_____

NOTES

NOTES

NOTES

NOTES

NOTES

www.ingramcontent.com/pod-product-compliance
Lightning Source LLC
Chambersburg PA
CBHW041428120626
46547CB00002B/136